WHAT WE FOUND THERE

First published in 2013
The Dedalus Press
13 Moyclare Road
Baldoyle
Dublin 13
Ireland

www.dedaluspress.com

ISBN 978 1 906614 86 7 (paperback)

Dedalus Press titles are represented in the UK by
Central Books, 99 Wallis Road, London E9 5LN
and in North America by Syracuse University Press, Inc.,
621 Skytop Road, Suite 110, Syracuse, New York 13244.

The Dedalus Press receives financial assistance from
The Arts Council / An Chomhairle Ealaíon

WHAT WE FOUND THERE

Poets Respond to the Treasures of
The National Museum of Ireland
Ard-Mhúsaem na hÉireann

Edited by
THEO DORGAN

DEDALUS PRESS
DUBLIN, IRELAND

Contents

for Dr. Pat Wallace, passionate steward

INTRODUCTION

❧

A MUSEUM, from the Greek *mouseion*, is, was or should be a temple of the Muses, a place where the attention is gathered and contemplation achieved, so that the divine lightning of inspiration may strike. This, or something like it, is what Pat Boran and myself had in mind when it occurred to us to ask a selection of poets to consider the collections of the National Museum of Ireland / Ard-Mhúsaem na hÉireann, with a view to embedding in a poem what reflective insight might prompt.

More prosaically, we asked our poets to respond to an object in the Museum's collections that spoke to them, that had come to inhere in memory, something that had in some sense or another acquired in their memories and imaginations a talismanic weight.

Many of the poems in this anthology do indeed cohere around an identifiable object, and it is not without interest that a number of poets have been drawn to the same object, but a number of others surprised me by addressing not an object but the museum itself, or even the idea of the museum.

I suppose I should not be surprised that in an age of information overload, where we struggle to stay conscious in the face of swarming clouds of ephemera, reflective minds should be drawn to objects that have somehow survived time and to the institutions that offer such objects safe haven.

Nuala Ní Dhomhnaill has a luminous phrase in her poem 'Ceist na Teangan':

Cuirim mo dhóchas ar snámh
i mbáidín teangan

I set my hope afloat / in a small boat of language — and like poems, those objects that speak to us of the past are afloat in the currents and eddies of time and chance. It is the one dance of time and circumstance that bears up both poem and object, and there is a terrible poignancy in the thought that this torc, say, or that poem, should be wholly itself and also a sign of so many cognate poems or objects that have sunk out of the story, will never be seen or heard of again.

The verb 'to muse' comes not from the Greek, as you might well think, and has nothing to do, at least nothing directly to do, with the term *mouseion*. It comes from the Old French *muser*, which comes into Middle English as carrying the meaning 'meditate'. It also, refreshingly enough, can mean 'to waste time'. Its primary contemporary meanings, as given in the OED, are: "be absorbed in thought; meditate continuously in silence; ponder" — and also: "Be affected with astonishment or surprise; wonder; marvel, *(at)*."

I like to think of our poets musing in the Museum, putting themselves in the way of whatever lightning might strike, might set the words moving and shaping themselves. I like to think of the rich variety of things that, saved from the dark nothingness by luck or by gifted scholarship, have been sitting or hanging or standing around in the Museum's halls, there, simply being themselves, waiting until some chance mind might strike suddenly into the heart of meaning and set the darkness echoing.

Time in a poem is time of the ancestors and the inheritors, geological time co-existing with time yet to come. In a museum, that compression is the heart of the matter: we look in time present on what has come down to us from the past, arrested a moment on its flight into the future.

I am glad that so many mysterious treasures have sparked into life in so many poems, and I am glad, too, that some of our poets have been charmed into words by the Museum itself in its various guises and manifestations. As much as anything else, this neighbourly gesture from one set of guardians, the guardians of memory in language, allows us all to salute and honour another set of guardians, the Museum curators, scholars and staff who preserve and nurture our treasure hoard, the memory and phenomena of our natural and our made, particular world.

We might wish to think of the Museum as an anthology of found poems, and of this little book as a museum in miniature, a mind palace full of discovered, speaking treasures. Walking the museum, book in hand, we might like to think of the place each of us, visitor and reader alike, has yet to play in taking the long conversation out into the unknown future. In any case, I hope that these poems, to whose authors I am very grateful, may shine some unexpected light on a national institution of which Ireland may justly be proud.

— Theo Dorgan

MICHAEL SMITH

Trinity of Faces

i.m. Brian Coffey

'The head of this three-faced man
on its statuary plinth
could be that of a poet,' Brian says,
left, right and centre,
his vision focused as needs be
but equally peripheral.

The poet as witness,
storer of memories,
adept in the tricks of memories,
the subjective dictates of feelings,
the ambiguity of language,
still always persistent in self-honesty
and the larger truths
of the void or redemption.

He looks at us now,
stony-faced.
And we try to imagine
what he saw and felt,
what gods or kings were his,
what events he witnessed.

We reinvent him now
in our own image,
using the blankness of ignorance.

The curator modestly speculates:
'It may be the face of an unknown god.'

MICHAEL LONGLEY

The Broighter Boat

A friend wears as a brooch
Gold boat, gold oars,
Refinement intensified
Below her breastbone,

Mast, oars, tiller
Hammered thin as ash
Keys, sycamore wings,
Rowlocks whispering,

Her journey's replica
With me a stowaway,
A transubstantial
Imaginary oarsman.

JOHN F. DEANE

Museum of Country Life

On the hither bank of the dark river, Methuselah-the-Heron
stood, the flow of minute, nor day, nor season
bothering him; this side the river, Patrick's high round tower

guards the dead against all weathering; across the water
the demesne, Big House, where I take the lift (its chrome
fittings, its engaging mirror) down out of the present, step

out into Granny's scullery, and there she is! sitting
on a wobbledy three-leggedy stool, the hour-glass churn
held like an unwilling child between her knees; black apron

with its smattering of stars, her grey hair wisping
down on her heated face, and she plunges and plunges,
churning; there is buttermilk in the bruised enamel
        bucket

where I dip a chipped Irel-coffee porringer to drink; on
        the floor
last night's scoured-out rose-patterned chamber-pot, and
        on the shelf
the great tureens with grey-blue willows, eternal flight

of rust-brown swallows on a rust-brown sky. 'Run,' she
        tells me,
'tell your granddad the spuds are in the pot;' I make, gently,
soft-heel, genteel half-turns and there I am at once, away

beyond the crossroads at Cafferky's roadside forge,
our big mule Romeo heaving at the ropes; Granddad
has his big fob watch, he has opened the jacket

of his RIC uniform, he is smoking his white clay pipe
and packing tobacco down with his big hard thumb;
he points, saying the words for me, tongs, croppers and
      hammers

and there — collar and hames, bridle and reins; we are
      standing hot
in a racket-hall livid with fire, there is anvil-ding and
      round-punch-dong,
hiss-swish-swash of steam when the red-hot shoe is
      whooshing down

into the basin, and misery! the sudden wuthering roar
of the ass; Cafferky, small and skinny, grinning nails,
is sporting his liver-coloured leathern apron to withstand
      all wars;

'Have you done,' says Granddad, spitting down into the
      flames,
'your homework?' and I make, gently, soft-heel genteel
      half-turns
and there I am in the Achill schoolroom, nailed boots

and rolled-down socks, trousers to the knee, all of us
      boys
awed and silenced before the vast expanse of the world
      beyond,
slates and chalk on the long desks, nib and inkwell and
      headline

copybooks, and I will forge out words, and plunge down
    deep
into language, I will fill copies, and pattern sentences
    into shape
in stitched and covered books. I was born here, will die,
    but will be

forever. I took the lift again, reluctantly, up to the
    present.
Outside, in a western mist, a long-eared owl let out its
    cry, obstinate
as a rusty hinge, from a high branch in the age-old pines.

Turlough, Castlebar, Co Mayo

THOMAS McCARTHY

Eileen Gray at The National Museum

If it was not chrome
It would have been stone,
Eileen Gray,
As everything good
Was neo-Classical stone
In your Irish Book of Common Prayer:
And if not stone, lacquer —
As Yves St. Laurent
Was lacquer in a Parisian life
So beautiful
You made him sit upon
A minimalist Wexford chair
And sip with delicate lips
From your table of chrome
That sits now in Collins Barracks;
Chrome as formal and pure
As a windblown egret:
Chrome as the prayerful lips
Of our National Museum.

MOYA CANNON

Molaise

Odd that he should be quartered here
where regiments mustered and marched
and orders were barked at straight-backed men.
His gaze has outlasted sword and fire —
the quiet gaze that fell for seven centuries
on the lintel and jambs of his stone house
and — when he was carried out, shoulder high —
on Sliabh Liag, Ben Bulben and Knocknarea,
on the deep walls and the speckled stones
of Inishmurray, where pilgrims made their stations
hoping to shed their agitation, if not their cares.

What drew me to this stillness
on many damp Dublin Saturdays,
my spirit at seventeen or twenty
a turbulence, a lurching boat?
I knew nothing of stormy Inishmurray,
with its monks and poitín-makers,
but was drawn to the oak sculpture
with the cheekbones of an Asian sage.
Sages were almost as suspect to me as saints
but Molaise was quiet as a Henry Moore
and touched the same ground in me.

And who was the artist who carved it
seven centuries after the saint's death? —
seven centuries after the battle at Ben Bulben,
over a book's copyright, and after, legend asserts,
Colmcille had come to Molaise in remorse

to receive a penance of green martyrdom
which sent him to Iona in the north.

Where did the sculptor learn his art?
And who was the commissioning abbot?
— anxious, perhaps, to draw a pilgrim trade
away from Armagh, Derry or Lough Derg —
a businessman maybe, who dealt
in curses and blessings, or maybe not,
for the corrupt middle ages were also the age
of Francis who listened to wolves and birds,
of Hildegard who left us songs,
of Julian who tells us 'All shall be well'.

There are people who transcend their time
to bring gentleness into a battered world,
and I, now in my middle age, am past denying
that I have known women and men
in whose presence I have been calmed and blessed,
under whose compassionate gaze I feel complete
as the storm-rounded stones on Inishmurray's coast.

GERALD DAWE

Torc

One late smoggy afternoon
the boys visit the National Museum,
crowding around treasured artefacts.

Everything seems ancient
in this peppery light;
soft voices, closing doors.

They shift from case to case,
foot to foot — flint heads, Celtic crosses,
the implements in their proper places.

Under all those forgotten faces
a simple arc of sun, the torc's beaten gold
like nothing seen before or since.

The Yellow Vase

What say you to a window sill
in the Ceramics Hall, to angling it
between the minutes to either side
of the sun being certainly up?

To letting it tell no story but its own?
To give no label, so porcelain snatches
of sunlight and cloud be
its only inkling of real worlds?

Tapered onto its very mouth,
as though having only a single chance
to take from ballast
what needs matter most,

its emptiness, the certainty of this.
In the signal abeyance a body gifts
to the historical world, what is hoarded,
I ask you, and what offered, what released?

Grant this vase, between us both,
the shape of all desire. Have it stand
so light discloses every nerve
and membrane in its being.

Say the glaze must hold still;
the gold forget what it cannot contain
of blood or disappointment.
Say its open mouth must be

an antonym to every flower
kept from it all this while.
Say the space that you vacate,
I enter, wordlessly,

as if longing could be an end in itself,
the yellow fact of it being, finally,
something to open in sunlight,
something to hold against time.

SINÉAD MORRISSEY

The House of Osiris in the Field of Reeds

I'm turning forty. Not on my birthday
(still, as I write, six weeks away) but over months.
It's like a migraine: that sludgy disconnectedness
starting in the brain, hours before the hammering.
I've forgotten my name and my husband's name
in the run-up to the full-scale meltdown.

All through last winter, each day
made to bear the pressure of impending loss.
Soon it will no longer be like this. The lean girls
picnicking in the park, their haul of charity-shop
dresses at their feet, listening to The Smiths,
have long since picked themselves up and vanished

down the tall-grass corridor of rooks and smoke.
I can no longer remember their faces, or what
the sky over Dublin inscribed on my skin
the year I'd just left home, or even the impact
of first-time, proper sex, of being unwrapped.
But turning forty banishes my younger self

to a separate outhouse, somewhere stony
and impassable, hot, fly-infested, like the city
of Tetu on the Nile which became The Otherworld
for all of Egypt, and I cannot get across.
Death was so much closer then, of course —
I'd be dead already or at least a grandmother,

if rich, I'd have my orders pre-prepared
for the sarcophagus maker, the Shabti carver,
the weaver of the shroud, I'd have selected
the spells for my coffin-lid, the amulets required
to survive the guarded entrances of the afterlife,
the tricky test with hearts and feathers.

O exiled one, so you may escape the heat
and torpor of that barren place, and pass instead
to the Field of Reeds, and do no work there,
discover by your grave cloths a replica of yourself
in turquoise faience, fashioned with a basket.
Here, it says. I'll do it. Take me.

MACDARA WOODS

Collins Barracks: Marching Orders

Above the vastness
Of the Barracks Square
The further vastness of the sky:
Eternal invitation to the party with Van Gogh
Without the organ stops
To celebrate the glittering air
Almost too fresh to breathe

But this is what you see
From prison too
Congealed behind grey walls —
To be surrounded by an emptiness so personal
So absolute
That it defies all falling into it
This side of madness

That imaginary place
Where non-existent circles intersect
To leave you
Dropping perpendiculars and tangents
To railway tracks
And tramlines
In the cobbled streets below

The Luas grand inquisitor
On the tram to Drimnagh asked
Howaya Chief …What age are you?
Not yet old enough
For travelling backwards in a stationary chair

Looking out the window
At the garden of the hospice
I am visiting today in Esher

Where everyone is free to walk outside
In summer
Or to be wheeled or walk outside in winter
Well wrapped up —
But old enough that everything that is is perilous
Foreseen and transitory
As guarded as a barracks square

And yet the marvellous wasteful
Momentary roundness
Of the Spring:
A woman running down her steps just now
Across the road
In pink pajamas
All shifting globes and bulbs
And soft tectonic plates accented

Seems airborne in the light of Richmond
Showing for an instant
How it can be done
To be waiting always to be ambushed by surprise
Unplanned
Remembering at seventy to breathe
Each fresh and glittering breeze into the lungs

BRIAN LYNCH

The Blaschka Radiolarian

for Killian Schurmann, glassmaker

The Blaschka radiolarian radiates joy.
That last word is a value judgment call.
It is invisible to the naked eye.

What grief is for is still unclear,
But sorrow on this scale would kill.
Its sun-burst energy is nuclear.
Born to whirl, it turns upon the edge
Between the limit and the charge,
And when it dies off all that's left
Remains an oceanic skeleton,
An empty cell, a star adrift,
A prison ship where out is in.

Compacted then as chert, a cemetery
Of thought, abandoned wrecks,
Of flotsam, jetsam, lagan, long stopped clocks,
Its membrane is its memory.

The self is what the self recalls;
Yet, as within the after daze of sex,
The trace effect of blues and golds
That love leaves when the lover goes,
It mimics, micro wise, in minerals,
Silica, silicate, siliceous.
Die-away-delicate joy wishes.

DERMOT HEALY

The Corleck Stone

in memory of Tom Barron, historian,
who introduced the Museum to the Stone

Out of the early Iron Age
The 3-faced stone head
That once stood looking
Over East Cavan

Now stands guard
As guide and interpreter
At the entrance to the Treasury.
One face is studying the antiquities

In a long mute gaze into the past —
The necklaces, the horse bits
The bronze bracelets —
While the second welcomes

The visitors in from the future
With a tight smile
And lowered eyes
As the third

Faces into the absurd
And the far beyond
Where Tom Barron
Stands in the shadows.

It was claimed
There had been a fourth face
On the top of the head
Looking up into the heavens

Staring at the flame
And though it's gone
It's still there
In the depths and pulses of consciousness

As the humble ghosts
Go to and fro
Across the fields
And time again

Shoots up
Through the hole in the lip
With a whistle,
As Master Barron sets off

Again astride a stone horse
On another journey
Into history
Surrounded by honeyed bees.

MARK ROPER

Great Northern Diver

I know you from the Rinnashark,
a single, solemn, dull, heavy bird,
eking out brief winter days in silence,
an ashy skulker in a channel.

A ghost of the shining example
by the door in the Dead Zoo:
a male bright in the summer plumage
we shouldn't see, colours that ripen

like a night sky when it leaves to breed
on a lonely American lake,
black back stamped with stars,
white stones strung round the throat.

The voice of a Creator echoed across
a void, found itself embodied
in shadow, spirit of this bird.
Sun saw the shadow, splashed it with light.

It calls in the quiet of evening,
a drawn-out, mournful haunt:
a lament for something lost long ago,
something never to be found again.

In its cabinet rising to the occasion,
looking down on lesser divers
to each side, lording it over petrel,
razorbill, shearwater and guillemot.

Rising from the past with the shoals of skin
and herds of fur, red deer all air and bone;
the half-creatures here to greet us
from a land between life and death.

Watching small feet wear out the tiles,
listening to the children chant as they leave:
Bye Otters, Bye Hares, Bye Sun Fish, Bye Whale,
Bye-bye Badger, Bye-bye Diver, Bye-bye Seal.

COLM BREATHNACH

Long

Amach as bád a thánamar go léir,
Long a sheol léi thar toinn.
Crann barrchaol feistithe innti
A ghlac brí ón ngaoith
Is a shéid anam i gclí na ndaoine
Ina suí istigh ina bolg thíos.

As cleite báidín chruinn
A thánas-sa i dtír.

Bád ocht seas is seacht rámh
Fan gach sleas agus ceann spártha
I gcúl an chlébhoird uirthi.
Bád gur shín stiúir fhada
Stuama isteach sa chúltsruth
As a deireadh.

Bímid go léir ag teacht i dtír
De shíor mar chine daoine,

I dtír in iath seo luí na gréine
Nó ar thalamh críoch i gcéin
Is ní sia a fhanfaidh an rian
A fhágfaimid inár ndiaidh

Ná
Rian éin ar chraoibh,
Rian fir ar mhnaoi,
Rian loinge ar an dtoinn.

A Ship

Every one of us came by boat,
A ship that sailed the waves over,
Fitted with a tapering mast
That passed vigour from the wind
Into the flesh of the people
Seated in the hold below.

From a featherlike little round boat
I came ashore.

A boat that had eight thwarts and seven oars
Along each side with one to spare
At the rear to port.
A boat with a long steady rudder
Stretching aft
From the stern.

As a race we are all
Forever making landfall

In this sundown land
Or in far-away places,
And the trace we leave behind
Will no more last

Than
The trace of a bird on a branch,
The trace of a man on a woman,
The trace of a ship on the ocean.

Amach as báidín beag beosach
Comair óir,
Mar a bheadh i gcás gloine sa mhúsaem,
A thánamar go léir.

Out of a small boat
Neat and trim and golden,
As if in a glass cage in the museum,
Every last one of us came.

Translated by the author

TONY CURTIS

Blessing on Things Made Well

Michael Egan made a set of uilleann pipes
In 1850. Now they lie silent in a glass display
Case at the Museum of Country Life

Under a sign that says:
Approximately in the key of C.
I love the beauty of those words.

You can't but admire the care and precision
Michael put into making these pipes —
As tuned to this life as possible.

For isn't everything, if looked at closely,
A little off key: lovers and dancers,
Only a step out, a step away;

Talkers on the tips of their tongues;
Towns at no distance;
Doors and drinkers slightly ajar.

I'd like a copy of that sign to hang on my wall.
Especially in winter, when the poems are buckled, bent;
Every one of them, *Approximately in the key of C.*

PATRICK DEELEY

Natural History

The last act of the huge pike — to swallow almost whole
a smaller rival. Which, before it dies, digs its way
half-through the gills of its attacker. Both specimens

float now in a formaldehyde jar, conflicted in one hunger
and one space for us to abhor, or find the nerve
to admire. Or there's a spaghetti ball of thread worms

extricated from the gizzard of another creature,
inducing a shudder. Or a wasp that makes a living larder
of the tarantula, so its own larva may survive.

On and on the dreadful devices, the live-or-die scenarios,
until we wonder if all's a case of cannibal existence
precluding redemption, and are shaken — as Darwin was —

out of the consoling notion of God as benign apotheosis
to which we aspire. Throw warfare into the hat,
throw barbarities we wage against earth and each other,

still somehow our morose hearts hold there exists a heaven
beyond the sway of instinct and natural wildness,
beyond the special sorrow saved for us, the aspirant angels.

CELIA DE FRÉINE

Gúna Lae

Gach uair agus mé ag feitheamh
ní ar an mbreith a dhírím
ach ar an ngúna
ar dhubh a lása

ar dhearg a shróil
ar bhán a fhosciorta
ainneoin cé chomh deacair is atá sé
dearmad a dhéanamh

ar an achar ama
ar an leaba luí seoil
is níos deacra fós
ar oíche an fhíona

Dar leis an sagart ba chóir
fáil réidh lena leithéid de smaointe
is cuimhneamh ar thoil Dé
ar shláine na bpáistí

Is orthu a smaoiním   ar ndóigh
ar a mbéilíní ar   a sonas
ach cuimhním ar an sonas eile
dhá mhí tar éis dom an leanbh a shaolú

nuair a tharraingeoidh mé orm an gúna seo
is a sheasfaidh mé
os comhair an scátháin
comair néata mar a bhí ariamh

Day Gown

Each time as I wait
it isn't on the birth I focus
but on the dress
on the black of its lace

the red of its satin
the white of its underskirt
in spite of how hard it is
to forget

the length of time
the childbirth
even harder to forget
the night of wine

According to the priest
we should put paid to these thoughts
and remember the will of God
the well-being of the children

Of course   I think of them
of their little mouths   their happiness
but I think of that other happiness
two months after the child is born

when I'll pull on this dress
and stand before the mirror
neat and trim
as ever

Agus tar éis dom a bheith coisricthe
is é mo ghúna
a bheidh bródúil
as sithiúlacht a lása is a shróil

And later when I have been churched
it'll be my dress
that'll take pride
in the stamina of its lace and satin

Translated by the author

KATIE DONOVAN

Woman Solstice

On the longest day
head bursting with hidden thunder
I go to find icons.
I am bleeding
bruised red petals,
and thinking of old bones;
new cries.
The sheela-na-gigs
lie in a dank crypt
flanked by ogham stones
and carved shards,
tagged and crumbling.
The sheelas squat on shelves —
forgotten; defiant.
One opens her legs
in a glaze of red,
one mocks death
with a thick glare
and a thrusting tongue.
Another gives herself joy
with a finger
on her pleasure pulse.
Some are featureless,
breastless,
but all open knees
pulling wide labia
with large, insistent hands.

They dare the eye to recoil.

The longest day
throbs to an end
blue light fading slow;
as I watch the roll
of the moon's disc
behind gathering clouds,
I am lying on cool sheets
splay-thighed
and smiling.

KERRY HARDIE

The Sunfish or Common Mola
in The Natural History Museum, Dublin

After thirty years I am back, visiting,
staring into the round glass eye of a fish
at once so weird and so enormous it's astounding
that the word 'common' forms part of its name.

It's here on the right in the same place.
This fish, called a sun fish or common mola,
has been gliding effortlessly down this gallery
since it was hauled from Lough Swilly in 1888,

the date someone wrote on its label
(though the scholarly hand that made the identification,
not being stuffed, mounted, touched up from time to time,
will long since have crumbled away).

I used to swim in Lough Swilly myself.
Had I known this gigantic dinner plate
(with its stubby fins extended, taller than I am)
might be waiting to rise from the depths

to sunbathe on top of the waves,
that its horned mouth might hoover my hair,
floating like the trailing stings of jellyfish —
I'd have been frightened witless.

Now it's swimming through time and this quiet museum,
round the back of those treasure-rooms gleaming with gold
that awe and amaze in Kildare Street —
Croziers and chalices. Bog-bodies. Torcs.

Fragments of bone in clay urns.
These rooms display the treasure we forget:
seabirds and songbirds, winging the bright air,
furred creatures, scuttling ancient woods and fields.

SEÁN LYSAGHT

A Brush for Auntie May

This small bundle of heather
tied with twine
is still sweeping ash
around her turf fire

and misses a ciaróg,
which escapes across the floor
to the shady scullery.
May's poultry hung there

in birth smells of water,
zinc and iron,
and the cattle reek
of her milking apron.

Her pride measured
a space of welcome
in brush strokes
across the Sunday hearth,

then broke a lit sod
with the beak of tongs
to make a griddle nest.
Her bread would bake and rise,

and be broken like a heart.
All gone now, of course,
except there's time after tea
for my mother to lift me

from my basket
and give me to her sister
in a perfect piece of allegory:
The Nation delivers her baby

to the raw hands of Care,
who exaggerates the hold
in her frame of shoulders,
and never lets me fall.

AIFRIC Mac AODHA

An Ialtóg

do Will Eno

I seile an sciatháin leathair,
Tá ceimiceán a choisceann
An fhuil ó théachtadh:

Ní hé an t-ainmhí as féin
Ná an duine ach oiread
Máthair oilc an ghreama
Ná sealbhaí na créachta.

The Bat

In the saliva of the bat
there is a chemical
that prevents coagulation.

Neither the animal alone
nor any person either
is the wound's source —
nor, indeed, its bearer.

Translated by Theo Dorgan

FRANK McGUINNESS

Furniture

for Eileen Gray

Count me among the fallen.

The story of my sins
May be contained in wood.
I opened my brown boots
And smelt the stains of linseed.
My eyes shed seven tears,
See if you can count them.
Blowing my stash of doubloons,
I shared my mug of arrach.
I squashed the fruit of Asia,
Dousing the Pyrenees.
I planted in its forests
What it is I seem to be —
The story of my sins,
A furniture of gallows.

Count me among the fallen.

CAITRÍONA NÍ CHLÉIRCHÍN

Taisce Bhrú Íochtair, Co. Dhoire 1ú hAois R.Ch.

Trín ghloine, chím múnla de bhád óir,
le crann, binsí ramhaíochta, rámhaí —
mionbhád is mionchoire óir
muince shármhaisithe,
coileár feadáin, péire coiléar casta toirc,
péire slabhraí muiníl
is torc óir de dhéanamh na Rómhánach

Réada a cuireadh i dtaisce mar ofráil
chuig Dia Mara na gCeilteach,
Manannán Mac Lir

I lár an Ard-Mhúsaeim
leánn a bhfuil thart orm
is deirim an ortha seo:

1. ORTHA DO MHANANNÁN

Tabhair amach ar bharr na dtonn mé,
a Mhanannáin, slánaigh mé
tabhair isteach sa bháidín órbhuí leat mé
a Dhia na Mara.

Ba mhéanar gabháil faoi thoinn leat
go Brú Íochtair, taobh le Loch Fheabhail
i do charbad thar an mhuir ghlan
go Magh Meall.

The Broighter Hoard, Co Derry, 1st Century BC

Behind the glass a boat of gold
Mast, gunnels, oars —
A small cauldron of a vessel
Exquisite in design, a jewel.

Tubes fashioned to the collar
Twisted torcs and neck chains
A golden band of Roman bend
Adorned á la Tène with lotus flower.

Offerings to Manannán Mac Lir
Here in the National Museum
These treasures about me fade
As I whisper this prayer:

1. PRAYER TO MANANNÁN

Deliver me out over the breaking waves
Great Manannán, away from this place of tears
Steer me safe in your boat of yellow gold
Enfold me, O Lord of the sea.

My desire is to charge the waves with you
To Broighter where the Foyle falls low
In your chariot over clear green seas
And on to Maigh Meall.

Ar nós mairnéalaigh
cuirfidh mé caora an chrainn sceiche
isteach sa tsáile ag lorg do chosanta
a Mhanannáin, i gcoinne na stoirme.

Lí na farraige farat
gabhra lir ag rith in éineacht leat
do chapall Enbharr mar each fúinn
tabhair foscadh dom, a Mhanannáin

Guthanna na farraige
is do ghuth féin ag iomramh ionam
d'fhionnrith airgid, de dhréimire óir,
imímis linn

Go stuama, bímis ag iomramh
ní fada go tír na mBan
ar Eamhain le hildath Féile
a bheas ár dtriall roimh fhuineadh gréine

Is d'achan eachruathar, iomghaoth
beidh ár dtriall go hoileán gan bhrón
gan easpa, gan gheimhreadh, gan fhulaingt
go Magh Réin i bhfad i gcéin

Like a sailor who casts
Hopeful haw berries to the tide
I will plead your protection Manannán
Against the creeping squall.

Your father's hounds run apace
Licking about you the foamy wake
Of Enbharr your crashing steed
Shelter me Great Manannán.

In your voice the shouting sea
Heaving like oars within me
Your silver gallop, your golden mane
Flying from the rip tides of life.

Let us row with steady hands
It is not far to the land of women
By sunset we will see
The wonders and welcomes of Eamhain

Your steed-charge to me is a whirlwind
Sending want and winter gusting
Our goal is an island of gladness
Magh Réin so far away.

Translated by Prionsias Mac a'Bhaird

MARY O'DONNELL

Old Croghan Man Knocking at the Window

He dined sublimely — elk and venison,
fat cattle grazed on green slopes at forest's edge;
all the help he needed to sow and till,
to hunt with hounds, bring home his pledge

of bounty. But they descended like a pack of wild dogs,
flailed him, then competed for his killing.
Trimmed cuticles and ovoid fingernails,
they left alone. Those fingers knew honour,

not labour; digits flexed to receive lord and crone
alike, to raise a spear, a goblet, a pouch of coins.
They broke everything else in his body: did he shriek
from loss of nerve? Nipples cut, upper arms riven

to thread his pain in hazel withies? Enough torment,
before they severed him in half? Poor king, failed king,
wedded to a harsh goddess of land and war,
fertility and death. No tyrant,

but a man who offended the people's mood,
put tidy fingernails on the day's agenda,
failing them and his goddess.
Or, perhaps there was famine.

At night, his fingernails come tapping
at the window of dreams, the filed strength of them.
By day, in the glass box of consciousness,
we witness fingers at rest, as if in sleep.

NESSA O'MAHONY

Notes for an Exhibit

Spotfin Porcupine Fish, Cuba 1991,
D.J. O'Mahony, MI31.1992

It catches the eye:
half globe, half water-mine,
outrage suspended
in display case 781 Vertebrata Pisces
on the first floor landing.

When threatened, it doubles in size,
swallows air and water, bristles spines,
sends neurotoxins till each tip sizzles
with venom more potent than cyanide.
Still netted all the same,
(there is no armour against fate)
transformed to artefact,
presented in great state
to one who'd done some service.

What else need we know?
That it spent a year
atop a china cabinet,
caught dust, snagged cloth?
That it was the extra guest
at many a family party?
That, seeing it encased,
a grandson made an excited phone-call?
A six-inch black-type card
acknowledges the donor
of whom little is known;
his dates are found elsewhere.

LIAM Ó MUIRTHILE

Bearnaí

Is fearr go mór
sampla an mhanaigh
i mbun na salm
a leanúint
agus ligint don tsamhlaíocht
dul ar fán,

an dán
a bhí sa cheann
ó thúis
a chuaigh i sáinn
le práinn a thromchúise
a bhineáil.

Faoiseamh iomlán.
Seo liom arís
isteach sa tír aineoil
lán d'fhocail gan bhrí,
gan buntagairt léarscáile
gan buntéacs iomlán
ach frása éigin i gcúl an chinn

a aithním, ar éigean,
ar chuair na habhann
a théann ar lár sa loch
a thagann chun cinn
arís sa ghleann
nó fé chló aibítireach
gearrtha i bportach.

Gaps

It were better by far
to follow the monk's
way through the psalms
allow the imagination
to go roaming

Bin
the poem
that begins in the head
and gets bogged down
in its own dead weight

Total release.
Here we go again
into *terra incognita*
groping through meaningless words
no map co-ordinates
without one complete original text
except for some phrase
buried in the hinterland of the mind

Barely recognised
along bends in the river
swallowed up in a lake
mysteriously reappearing
in the valley
or in the guise of an alphabet
cut out of a bog.

Is iad na bearnaí fós
is léire a osclaíonn
is go hobann preabann
trí gach ceann acu amach
in valle lacrimarum ó m'óige
is dúnann le clocha paidrín
méar ar mhéar im ghlaic.

It is still the gaps
that reveal themselves the clearest
and suddenly through each breach
in valle lacrimarum from my youth jumps out
and they close with the stones of the beads
from finger to finger in my fist.

Translated by Gabriel Rosenstock with Liam Ó Muirthile

CATHAL Ó SEARCAIGH

Cailleacha na Feasa

do Aoife McGarrigle

Is beag an baol go dtitfeadh néal orm
na hoícheanta geimhridh adaí agus seanmhná
an bhaile ag airnéal i dtigh s'againne.

Iad ag cur tharstu cois tine, ag clabaireacht
is ag cúlchaint is ag cur thart an tsnaoisín
ó dhuine go duine sula dtosódh an taibhseoireacht.

Mhothóinnse an saol eile ar tinneall inár dtimpeall
agus cailleacha na clúide á tharraingt chucu go líofa.
Sa chisteanach ní allas taisligh a bhreacaigh na ballaí,

arrachtaigh a bhí ann á dtaibhsiú féin as béal an aeir.
Ag sealaíocht ar a chéile, d'aithris na mná a dtaithí
ar dheamhain agus ar spioraid, ar thaibhsí agus ar
        dhiabhail,

ar na mairbh a bhí ag siúil thart ina mbeatha i Mín a' Leá;
ar na cróchnaidí liatha a chífeá idir an dá sholas in Altán;
ar na hainspioraid a thriall bealaigh uaigneacha na hoíche
        i Mín na Craoibhe,

ar na deamhain aeir a bhí ag béicigh i mBeanna na Míne;
ar dhaoine beaga na Bealtaine a chuirfeadh tú ó mhaith;
ar na hanamacha fáin, tinte gealáin an tSeascainn Mhóir.

The Old Women Who Knew

for Aoife McGarrigle

There was no chance that I'd fall asleep
those winter nights when the old women
of the townland came rambling to our house.

They'd spread themselves around the fire, nattering
and gossiping and sending around the snuff
turn and turn about until the conjuring began.

I'd feel the other world straining all around us
and the old fireside women drawing it fluently out.
It wasn't condensation that dappled the kitchen walls,

it was spectres disgorging themselves out of the air.
One after the other the women told of their familiarity
with demons and spirits, with ghosts and with devils,

with the dead who walked alive in Mín a' Leá,
with the grey ghostly funerals you'd see in the half-light at
    Altán,
with the ghouls who travelled the lonely night-time ways
    in Mín na Craoibhe,

with the airy demons who were screeching in Beanna na
    Míne,
with the little people of Bealtaine who would lure you astray,
with the lost souls, the boggy phosphorescence of
    Seascann Mór.

Cé acu i mbarr an tsléibhe nó amuigh ar an réiteach
bhí bunadh an uaignis i réim go tréan is a ngleo le chlos
i bhfios do chách, a déarfadh na mná. Bhí an taer is an
    talamh beo leo.

Síofróga agus samhailteacha! Neacha éagsamhalta!
B'eol do na cailleacha go raibh gach ball den tsaol seo
faoi gheasracha dúrúnda ag an bheatha úd thall.

Bheadh daor orainn a chomharlaigh said go heolasach
mura ndéanfadh muid comharsantacht mhaith
le treabhchas an dorchadais a bhuanaigh inár measc.

Agus cé gur mhór mo dhúil ina gcuid scéalta scanrúil,
a gcuid taibhsí toirmisc is a dtithe siúil, thigeadh uamhan
an uaignis orm is na seanmhná a ndúiseacht is a
    dtabhairt chun solais.

Is d'fhágfaí mé, mar a ba ghnáth leo féin a rá agus iad i
    ndáil an bhrátha,
'chomh lag le malartán linbh, chomh lom le huisce marbh',
ag creathnú roimh neacha nár léir domh is roimh nithe a
    mhair i mbéal an aeir.

Agus b'iontach liom i dtólamh an dóigh a raibh siadsan
    in ann
lena gcuid orthaí cosanta agus a gcuid cleachtaí
    crábhaidh
an dá shaol bhagartha seo a thabhairt leo go beo.

Whether it was on the top of a mountain or out on the
    level ground
the tribe of loneliness was flourishing and their voices
    were to be heard
clearly by everybody, the old women would say. Earth
    and air were alive with them.

Fairy-women and phantoms! Unfathomable beings!
The old women knew that every single corner of this
    world
was spellbound in mystery by the life on the other side.

We would pay dearly, they counseled sagely,
if we were not bound by a neighbourly understanding
with the people of darkness who were settled among us.

And although I took great delight in their scary stories,
their poltergeists and their haunted houses, the terror
of loneliness came upon me as the old women drew
    them down towards the light.

And I'd be left, as they'd say themselves in the face of the
    final terror
'As weak as a changeling, as lifeless as standing water',
trembling before imperceptible beings and things that
    lived in the jaws of the air.

And I marveled always at how they were able
with their placatory charms and their pious practices
to escape with their lives from these two threatening
    worlds.

Is d'imeodh siad faoi dheireadh, seálta dubha casta
ar a gcloigne, a gcuid lampaí doininne ag déanamh
fios an bhealaigh daofa idir dhá dhorcha na hoíche.

Tchím iad anocht i m'aigne, an saol sin ag imeacht leo síos
an bóthar buan, fios feasa na beatha ina mbéala balbha;
cos amháin acu sa tsaol seo, cos eile sa tsíoraíocht.

And they'd leave in the end, their black shawls wrapped
tight around their heads, their storm-lanterns illuminating
the way before them in the deepest dark of the night.

I see them tonight with my mind's eye, that world
    disappearing with them
down the path of permanence, the inside-outs of life
    now forever unspoken;
one foot in this world, the other in the everlasting.

Translated by Paddy Bushe

PADRAIG ROONEY

Museum Pieces

i SLIOTAR

I stuffed this *sliotar* with my own hair,
from armpit and groin, chest and head.
Think of it as a perverse craft of exile.
When you puck it high into your air,
think of the hurlers of Mayo and Sligo
at Mayday hurling festivals pucking
the *sliotar róin* of love. Compact in it
our caresses, idle touches, frictions.
Weigh this love ball in your palm
and play with it. Think of me thinking
of you playing with it like before
when our love was hurley, pure hurley.

ii DOTAKU BELL

I've not lost my tongue.
Hear how sweetly I sounded
two millennia.

Though dumb and pendent,
struck, it all comes back to me
clear as the foundry.

A harvest bell rings
and they run across the fields
like sheaves, like the years.

iii THE PUTUMAYO MANIKIN

I wear this headdress of human scalps
hung with beetle wings and feathers
and this belt plaited with the skins
of red-billed toucans. Around my neck
are puma teeth and red beads, clicking.
What covers my groin are dried seeds,
snail shells, a see-through apron of feathers
and amulets with snakeskin edges.
On my arse are quills, threaded seeds,
macaw breast feathers, seedpods,
monkey teeth, beetle wings, toucan feathers.

I was brought from the Amazon basin
by Roger Casement, to be stared at.
He saw me as I am, bright with spoils
and tatters of hunting, warlike, beautiful.
I recognised him and cried: 'Take me
as a trophy wife, your bearer, your boy.
Expose me as a foundling in that far-off island.
Cover my nakedness with your own,
wear me as camouflage and armour.
I am the man still underneath your skin,
the one you sloughed off and forgot.'

GABRIEL ROSENSTOCK

Róba an tSagairt

Chuireas umam
Róba síoda an tsagairt
Labhraíonn an fia tríom
An grús
An toirtís
An nathair
Ollphéist
Agus dragain
Róba síoda an tsagairt
Chuireas umam
D'fhonn labhairt libh
D'fhonn labhairt libh
D'fhonn labhairt libh anois d'aonghuth

The Priest's Robe

I donned
The priest's silken robe
The deer speaks through me
The crane
Tortoise
Snake
A monster
Dragons
The priest's silken robe
I donned
To speak to you
To speak to you
To speak to you now with one voice

Translated by the author

AIDAN MURPHY

Elephant Skull

Here is a strange grail indeed!
A Cyclopean vessel with teeth,
a ponderous mass
bereft of flesh and ivory.

What monstrous apparition
imbibed from this gargantuan mug,
to leave it so parched

with a thirst
that all the world's tears —
past, present and to come —
will never slake.

BIDDY JENKINSON

Ard-Mhúsaem na hÉireann

Trí nithe atá ann
gan a bheith ann:
súil a d'aithin,
lámh a chaomhnaigh,
croí a chuir cuisle
in iarsmaí.

National Museum of Ireland

Three things there
and not there:
the seeing eye,
the cherishing hand,
the heart that found a pulse
in a relic.

Translated by Theo Dorgan

PADDY BUSHE

Hokusai's Tama River

There is struggle in this, the ferryman angled
Hard against his pole to hold the bow steady

Against wind and current. As always, he chooses
Fuji, dominant on the horizon, to be his mark.

He will, he knows, be carried broadside, downriver
Across his course. But the bow, he knows, will hold

Steady enough for today. The snow on Fuji's summit
Will be the same beacon it has always been.

Although the river is choppy, there are no waves
To threaten the daily struggle over and back.

The man watering his mule, on this side
Of the river, is reassured. The summit gleams.

MÁIGHRÉAD MEDBH

Hall of Two Truths
or
What the Dor Beetle Saw

(as she bustled round her galleries of eggs —
buried bombs — in the generative dung)

GHOST
three reflected lights on the zero-faced head.
impossible offspring, malformed, no thorax.
two legs trapped in the body, four legs frozen.
never had she felt such pure absence of flesh.
she would abort this polycarbonate snitch,
but it mirrored the desert hope of instar,
summoned her mind to its inviolate void.
she sat upon its limpid lap and listened.

moon in the black — guru — your geometry's a puzzle.
how can I measure — vacant eye — your worth and weight?

LENS
'in the rooms of louis fifteenth,' it chanted,
'chairs were made of cherry wood and fine brocade.
you scuttling labourers dared not land on them.
did you know that creatures like you are covered
in jewels and pinned to mexican blouses?'
she primed her legs for battle or quick retreat,
but lost direction on the polymeric field,
dust of hoof and cannon-smoke baffling her view.

in face of death — recurring absence — recall your nature.
half a billion years — dung-child — you've been delving.

HELMET
she turned to brass and was japanned, her wings trapped.
someone else's shell. an ornament indeed.
skin of the leopard that ate the fleur de lis
became her thorax. medusa was her horn.
a plume of horsehair, died red, swung behind her.
underbelly lice morphed to a splendid thing,
'first among war and women'. the beetle preened.
this was her wildest dream, a moult sublime.

head feeds on hat — saprophage — and hat on hope.
we advance — gasp or gallop — into monumental change.

IMAGO
the mount fell and all her body swelled with earth.
the officer lay dead, his last letter ripped.
but this was her element. she burrowed deep
and started tuning for a mate. no news came.
only bollywood radio on the air.
she drowned her sorrows in fetid swill and bopped.
civilisation marched on. another chair came down,
pressing her to a thin, hard coin.

the bardo — ghost pilgrim — is a dark mouth
it breathes you in — buried sun — and holds

GABRIEL FITZMAURICE

The Lislaughtin Cross

The world that constructed you
United prayer and art,
Now we live in a different world
That deconstructs the heart.

And still you stand before us,
Witness to a time
When man believed in symmetry
And art believed in rhyme

As I believe in symmetry
When I take up my cross
With the artists who before me
Drew beauty from life's dross.

CIARAN CARSON

Michael Collins: Three Items, in Order of Placement

handgun

tunic button

fountain pen

GRACE WELLS

Ten Chairs

There is little light-hearted
about these chairs. No!
These are serious chairs.
All ten of them. All different.
Chairs of oak and ash
and pine. One is a súgán chair
and one made entirely
of coiled straw.
These chairs came from a house
that was famous for music,
a house famous for stories,
and a house that no longer stands.

These chairs are dense
with the lean times, the hard times,
the times of danger
and the times of want.
They were scraped over flag-floors
that wept in certain weathers,
they were saved for Sundays,
they were the only chairs.
There must once have been
thousands of such chairs;
they must have gone
from circulation one by one.

Now in this room these chairs
are speaking oral history.
Pass round the clay pipes
let there be talk of rain
and how the dog fox has been
barking in the early dawn.
These chairs are the congregation
of a townland,
they know about laughter
and easy mirth. Later
they will be pushed back
for the dancing —

but remember there is little
light-hearted here,
only some playful aspect
in their arrangement —
row upon row —
reminds of a childhood game
where everyone must run
in a circle until the music stops
and you have to dive
for a chair,
except there are never enough
to go round.

It is after all a serious game
meant to teach us how fragile we are,
how precarious the fates,
how easy to be out of the running.

EILÉAN Ní CHUILLEANÁIN

The Gift

A hand rooted in a pocket —
Of leather and old fur, it seemed —
Jingled all the syllables till,
Reaching out, it offered the gift,
Then relaxed its hold: the girl's hand
Stretched and grasped. She kept it safely,
Walking, the three days and three nights
On the dry paths, past closed houses,
Fields of thistles and empty barns.
It was enfolded, covered, tucked
Neatly away in its Latin,
Clasp and hasp severe and entire.
The beasts embracing clenched their jaws,
The human-headed manticore
And the angels watched jealously.

She kept them from tearing her, nights
Repeating rhymes of ablatives,
Prepositions.
                    She saw a gate
Before her: there was work and food
And a place to sleep. She waited,
Still, for the urgent moment when
She would open the clasp, the day
When the deadlines could all go hang
While for still hours she turned pages
Till dark, reading the words out loud.

MARY O'MALLEY

Lunula

You want to finger it, try it on.
Just that, feel the soft light
On the throat.
It holds the world's shape.
It gave distinction, and rank.
Under the hill where they mined it
Bodies gleamed with flint and fire.

Sheet gold, cut by an expert.
Even the sound is aurum.
It strengthens
The Iberian connection,
The longing for sun,
A reserve we can depend on.
Made well, it lasts.

JOAN NEWMANN

The Keeper of the Sheilagh-na-Gig

A roomful of them.
A roomful of sheilaghs.
He smiles and we take a photo
of the keeper, his hand on the head
of S.G.4, as if she was his
unpredictable daughter. 'And
this is the smallest one.'
He shows us S.G.3
who hasn't quite got the hang
of exposing her pubes,
copying her sisters. They know
they are safe. That the keeper
is their father. That he will
not let them be taken —
that he will not let anyone
say anything bad about them.

KATE NEWMANN

Hollywood Stone: The Irish Labyrinth

It's not the Irish monk
glancing at a straggle of gorse
by the stone on the long path
to Glendalough,
shuddering at the womb shape,
chastising himself: think
of the winding road of life
ending in the true cross,
its second chance, its
power of resurrection …
sandals scuffling damp grass,
the clothy toll of his wet hem
against his shin.

It's Ariadne, after Theseus
has abandoned her on the Isle of Naxos,
thinking aloud how she always feared it,
the Minotaur, her half-brother
they had to bury from the light
but needed to hear. Howling
up from the dark he was
the rawest, gentlest, fiercest
muffled part of herself.

But Theseus had to kill it off,
use her to fight back out to the sun.
And the thread — his need of her,
her gift to him of the pulsing earth —
made him so angry. He said she'd changed.

And how could he live
after the labyrinth? How?
That atonal echo musicking his mind,
tilting him towards a shriek of madness.

It was when Theseus had felt his way in,
into the inner ear of rock —
left-side, right-side, through the torment of the brain
to the core of being.
The way when he entered her
they tremored into molten.
Then, when they really knew each other,
that was when the story should have ended.

GERARD SMYTH

The Collins Coat

Look at it now, the greatcoat worn by him
in the cloud weather of the south, in the assassin's
gimlet view. Imagine this — the sway

and swish of it, harp-buttons aglitter
as he made his way through the hiss of enmities,
clenched fists, the whispered and shouted

oaths of allegiance. Hard shoulders, long sleeves
fit for the arms he raised at the monster meetings
or when he was ready to sign on the dotted line:

death warrants, treaties. Thick wool of military green
worn into shape by a nation-builder's
girth — the cut of it a clear outline

filling its own glass shrine. And so it became
his shroud — this mantle, garment, sagging weight
of collar and hem, with pockets that once held

the wiles of war and peace, the gun in politics.

MICK DELAP

from **Bantry Bay**

> *Opening disposition of Lieutenant Proteau, officer*
> *commanding the Captain's gig of the French frigate 'Le*
> *Resolué'; the gig cast ashore on Bere Island, the 24th day of*
> *December, 1796.*

The slam-hold-glide, slam-hold-glide of ten oars pulling,
the men naked to the waist and showering sweat.
How they lifted her up with every stroke they took.
And how, long keeled and true, she flew along her course.

That was last summer, in Brest, where we built her.
And still gripped by this abominable Irish winter,
worst jailer of them all, I cherish the thought of her grace,
how lightly she waited, how freely she moved on the water.

The seine boats where I grew up, on a rocky coast like this,
had six great timber sweeps, two men to each;
twelve men to drag the purse around the glittering shoals,
and squeeze a pittance from the indifferent sea.

When we began to build, I knew I wanted more:
a sheerline that flowed unforced from stem to wine-glass
    stern,
twelve metres without an ugly bend along them,
that oars and creamy canvas would seduce to motion.

Monsieur le Capitane wanted style, and humoured my plans
as we laid down her oak keel and transom, built up her
    frames,
planked her in larch — nine carvel, two clinker —
finished her gunwhale in oak, and oarports in leather.

Launched, we stroked her joyously round the gathering
	fleet,
in weather M. Tone called more fit for May than December;
until, on the sixteenth of Frimaire we heaved her on board,
set sail, in gales that suddenly recalled mid-winter.

Snow mixed with spray, as the great ships lurched
and lumbered. Our rendezvous was Mizen Head,
but as we waited the 'Redoutable' burst from the murk,
and ran on board; in a ruin of cordage, smashed our
	bowsprit.

We jury rigged the foremast, checked the gig in its lashings,
and pumped for our lives, men and panting officers
alongside Ireland's brooding rebels, till we made Bantry
in the teeth of the gale, and got our anchor down off Bere.

Closing disposition of Lieutenant Proteau

By Christmas Eve, our 'Resolué' and all on board
were losing heart. It was a madness of sleet and gusts
that slammed down off the hills onto a sea so short and
	vicious
our cable snubbed and surged desperately against it,

till the hawse splintered, more planks began to start,
and in spite of her name we began to lose ground at the
	pumps.
The Captain wanted to pay her off by the head, cut the
	cable
and run out to sea. But without a bowsprit, we needed a tow.

The 'Immortalité' lay off to windward,
so in spite of the gale we readied the gig
with a triple-reefed main, our ten strongest oarsmen,
and four more, to bail, and help me with the helm.

She took off on a formidable charge South East across the
      Bay,
one moment surfing faster than any ship we'd known,
the next brought up all standing as she buried her bows
in a torrent of green that threatened to keep her heading
      on down.

Oh, she was superb, as we struggled to live with seas
no other ship's boat could have managed. But we made
      no ground
to windward, neither by sail nor oar, and tack by tack
we were forced further from the 'Resolué', further off shore.

As dusk came on, our condition was lamentable,
the men scarce able to cry out or move, the icy water
      gaining,
and each tack pushing us nearer the open sea's quietus.
Until in the gloom I caught sight of the mark you call
      Ardnakinna.

We made through Piper's Sound to Dinish, and gave
      ourselves up,
all but two who had already died. The rest will be pressed.
For myself, I do not care. But to lose the gig is bitter.
Whoever gets her, I envy him the joy I built into her.

PAULA MEEHAN

Old Fossil

*A meditation on tautology in The Natural History Museum,
Merrion Square*

To spin the bitter word, the bad review,
the slagging in the blog I am reading,
to charm a lifespan with bright coins of luck:
the flipside of the putdown *old fossil*
is to be shrined forever in cold stone,
to be read as tail, as fin, as feather
in some natural history museum

in some far off fin-de-millennium
fever in apocalyptic weather
when this sad world is dust; and my vain bones
endure as sigils on the post-ordeal
sea bed, posterity's primordial muck,
like trilobite, like brachiopod, dreaming
calamite — eternity's daft voodoo.

GERRY MURPHY

The Ghost of William of Orange
Considers his Gauntlets

Ah those gauntlets!
The funny thing is I had forgotten them
in the hurried preparations for battle.
My Aide-de-Camp noticed and rode back
to retrieve them before I had even missed them.
So, my theory of "lucky" gauntlets
still remains untested, since we had the victory.
A twelve hour struggle, but unfortunately
not the decisive battle we had hoped for.
Our main encircling tactic failed miserably,
most of James' army were able to retreat unmolested.
And instead of settling it there and then on the Boyne,
the war dragged on to more and bloodier encounters.
Our European allies celebrated,
with Te Deums being sung in Vienna and the Vatican.
The Pope himself no less, presiding in Rome.
My shock troops, the Dutch Blue Guard,
Catholics to a man, performed with their usual zeal.
I presented the gauntlets to John Dillon,
who hosted my officers and myself
in his magnificent castle after the battle.

FRED JOHNSTON

101 Uses for Straw

Some say there are one hundred-and-one uses for straw
A number round enough to have magic in it, or a brace
    of spells
It can be read backwards without losing its weight
But read straw the same way and you get warts —
Nonetheless, there are one hundred-and-one uses for straw

From a horse's bridle and bit to a rope to hang yourself
You pull it out the same for strength and length and tight
    lasting
The song says that twisting straw for rope
Can get rid of a teasing lover if he's foolish enough
These are some of the one hundred-and-one uses for straw

Rope's a good thing and useful in a hundred-and-one
    ways
But parcelled into the glass case are straw nooses
To remind you that rope's not for skipping or playing with
Or being idle or careless in handling, it's made for
    tying up
And killing too and wrapping a man's hands for the
    hang-rope

And out of the straw you'd otherwise toss on a flagged
    floor
A hundred-and-one purposes rise up, rope being the
    commonest —
A thing that has so many intents and designs
Is a wonder not made for hanging in a display case,
No more than you'd pin a eucharist or some small god
    to a wall.

NOTES and ACKNOWLEDGEMENTS

The National Museum of Ireland /Árd-Mhusaem na hÉireann is in Kildare Street, Dublin 2. There are collections of the Museum also in The Natural History Museum, Merrion Street, Dublin 2, in Collins Barracks, Benburb Street, Dublin 7, and in The Museum of Country Life, Turlough Park, County Mayo.

P. 13. Michael Smith, 'Trinity of Faces' A three-faced stone head in the National Museum, Kildare Street.

P. 15. Michael Longley, 'The Broighter Boat' A 20 cm gold boat in the National Museum, Kildare Street

P. 16. John F. Deane, 'Museum of Country Life'. The Museum itself is Deane's subject.

P. 19. Thomas McCarthy, 'Eileen Gray at The National Museum'. A chrome table in Collins Barracks

P. 20. Moya Cannon, 'Molaise'. $13^{th} - 14^{th}$ century carved oak figure of St. Molaise in the National Museum, Kildare Street.

P. 22. Gerald Dawe, 'Torc'. Gold ornament in the National Museum, Kildare Street.

P. 23. Vona Groarke, 'The Yellow Vase' Object Number: DC:1886.10547 Specimens of glazed pottery (1886.80 – 126). Modern Irish, by Vodrey, Dublin. Various sizes. By Frederick Vodrey, Moore Street, Dublin, c.1884.

P. 25. Sinéad Morrissey, 'The House of Osiris in the Field of Reeds'. Shabti display in the museum on Kildare Street — the funerary statuettes depicted with hoes and baskets so they could carry out the work required of the deceased in the afterlife.

P. 27. Macdara Woods, 'Collins Barracks: Marching Orders'. The Museum itself is Woods' subject.

P. 29. Brian Lynch, 'The Blaschka Radiolarian'. Radiolarians are microscopic ocean organisms. Laid down as sediment, they can become chert, a brittle rock used in pre-history to make knives and arrowheads. This greatly magnified model was made by Leopold Blaschka (1822-1895) and his only son Rudolf (1857-1939), Bohemian glassmakers of genius who worked in Dresden. The Natural History Museum owns some 500 examples of their work.

P. 30. Dermot Healy, 'The Corleck Stone'. Early Iron Age stone head in the National Museum, Kildare Street.

P. 32. Mark Roper, 'Great Northern Diver'. An exhibit in the Natural History Museum.

P. 34. Colm Breathnach, 'Long'. The Broighter Boat, in National Museum, Kildare Street.

P. 38. Tony Curtis, 'A Blessing on Things Made Well'. These pipes have since been moved to the Ulster Folk and Transport Museum. They were likely made in Liverpool, to where Egan the maker had emigrated.

P. 39. Patrick Deeley, 'Natural History'. Stuffed pike in Natural History Museum.

P. 40. Celia de Fréine, 'Gúna Lae'. Reference is to an exhibition in National Museum, Collins Barracks, *The Way We Wore,* and to an exhibit, a dress belonging to Mary Doyle which she wore after the birth of each of her ten children.

P. 44. Katie Donovan, 'Woman Solstice'. Reference is to cheerfully blatant stone carvings of figures exposing their vulvas, known as Sheela-na-gigs, in the National Museum, Kildare Street. Poem, from *Rootling: New & Selected Poems* (2010), by gracious permission of Bloodaxe Books

P. 46. Kerry Hardie, 'The Sunfish or Common Mola in The Natural History Museum, Dublin'. The ocean sunfish is the heaviest known bony fish in the world. Many of the sunfish's various names allude to its flattened shape. Its specific name, "mola", is Latin for "millstone". Its common English name, "sunfish", refers to the animal's habit of sunbathing at the surface of the water. Sunfish live on a diet that consists mainly of jellyfish.

P. 48. Seán Lysaght, 'A Brush for Auntie May'. Exhibit in the Museum of Country Life.

P. 50. Aifric Mac Aodha, 'An Ialtóg'. Stuffed bat on exhibit in Natural History Museum

P. 51. Frank McGuinness, 'Furniture'. Furniture by Eileen Gray, on show in National Museum, Collins Barracks.

P. 52. Caitrona Ní Chléirchín, 'Taisce Bhrú Íochtair, Co. Dhoire 1ú hAois R.Ch.' The Broighter Hoard, National Museum Kildare Street.

P. 56. Mary O'Donnell. 'Old Croghan Man Knocking at the Window'. Old Croghan Man was found in a bog beneath Croghan Hill in Co. Offaly. Based on radiocarbon dating he died sometime between 362 BCE and 175 BCE. In the National Museum, Kildare Street.

P. 57. Nessa O'Mahony, 'Notes for an Exhibit'. The spotfin porcupine fish (Kingdom, Animalia; Phylum, Chordata; Class, Actinopterygii; Order, Tetraodontiformes; Family, diodontidae; Species, hystrix). In the Natural History Museum.

P. 58. Liam Ó Muirthile, 'Bearnaí'. The Fadden More Psalter, an 8th century CE manuscript in The National Museum, Kildare Street.

P. 62. Cathal Ó Searcaigh, 'Cailleacha na Feasa'. Prompted by various domestic exhibits, particularly those pertaining to firesides, in the Museum of Country Life.

P. 70. Gabriel Rosenstock, 'Róba an tSagairt'. Daoist priest's robe in the Albert Bender Collection, National Museum at Collins Barracks.

P. 73. Biddy Jenkinson, 'Ard-Mhúsaem na hÉireann'. The National Museum itself is Jenkinson's subject.

P. 74. Paddy Bushe, 'Hokusai's Tama River'. The woodblock print is in the Bender collection in Collins Barracks, Catalogue number DB:1932.114.

P. 75. Máighréad Medbh, 'Hall of Two Truths'. The Exhibits: Location: Decorative Arts & History, Collins Barracks: Helmet of an officer of the Bengal Horse Artillery c.1845 (Soldiers and Chiefs, Floor 1). Louis Ghost Chair, by Philippe Starck, 2002. Transparent polycarbonate (Four Centuries of Furnishings). Location: Natural History Museum, Merrion Street: Dor beetle. Also known as: Lousy Watchman, Dumble-dor, Clock and Shardborne beetle.

P. 77. Gabriel Fitzmaurice, 'The Lislaughtin Cross'. A 15th century CE processional cross in the National Museum, Kildare Street.

P. 78. Ciaran Carson, 'Michael Collins: Three Items, In Order of Placement'. Once the Property of Michael Collins (Commander-in-Chief of the Irish National Army), Exhibited at the National Museum of Ireland, Decorative Arts and History Department, Collins Barracks (formerly the Royal Barracks), Dublin.

P. 79. Grace Wells, 'Ten Chairs'. In the Museum of Country Life.

P. 81. Eiléan Ní Chuilleanáin, 'The Gift'. Reference is to Fadden More Psalter, National Museum, Kildare Street.

P. 82. Mary O'Malley, 'Lunula'. A gold neck ornament in the National Museum, Kildare Street.

P. 83. Joan Newmann, 'The Keeper of the Sheilagh-na-Gig'. See entry for Katie Donovan above.

P. 84. Kate Newmann, 'Hollywood Stone: The Irish Labyrinth'. Stone with an incised labyrinth motif, found near the pilgrimage route known as St, Kevin's way, Glendalough, County Wicklow. In the National Museum, Kildare Street.

P. 86. Gerard Smyth, 'The Collins Coat'. Army greatcoat, once the property of General Michael Collins. National Museum at Collins Barracks.

P. 87. Mick Delap, *from* Bantry Bay'. The Bantry Longboat, a ship's gig dating back to the ill-fated French landings at Bantry, County Cork in 1796. In the National Museum at Collins Barracks.

P. 90. Paula Meehan, 'Old Fossil'. Irish fossils in the Natural History Museum.

P. 91. Gerry Murphy, 'The Ghost of William of Orange Considers his Gauntlets'. The gauntlets are in the National Museum, Collins Barracks.

P. 92 Fred Johnston, '101 Uses For Straw'. Exhibit in the Museum of Country Life.